VAN

**communication
skills for
couples**

little
book
series

First published 2008
Copyright © 2008
Reprinted 2010

British Library Cataloguing in Publication Data.
Catalogue record for this book is available from the
British Library.

ISBN 978-1-906381-02-8

Published by
Autumn House Limited, Grantham, Lincolnshire.

Printed in Thailand.

All texts are taken from the *New Living Translation*
(Tyndale House Publishers) unless indication is given to
the contrary. Other versions used include:

MGE = *The Message Bible*
RSV = *Revised Standard Version*
The Amplified Bible
NASV = *New American Standard Version*
KJV = *King James Version*

Communication is the Number One Marriage Problem

The happiness of a couple can be measured to a large degree by the effectiveness of their communication.
How a couple communicates is one of the most powerful factors affecting the success or failure of their relationship.

'The Christian wife brings holiness to her marriage, and the Christian husband brings holiness to his marriage. . . . Don't you wives realise that your husbands might be saved because of you? And don't you husbands realise that your wives might be saved because of you?'
1 Corinthians 7:14, 16

Listed in order of frequency
are the most common
marriage problems that
divide and push apart couples:

1. Breakdown in communication
2. Loss of shared goals and interests
3. Sexual incompatibility
4. Infidelity
5. Excitement and fun gone from
   relationship
6. Money
7. Conflicts over children
   8. Alcohol and drug abuse
   9. Women's rights issues
   10. In-laws

Notice that infidelity is in the number 4 spot.

Infidelity is usually not the real problem. It is the 'result' of other problems between a couple that commence with a communication breakdown.

Yesteryear's marriage was held together by the struggle for survival. Couples were concerned with providing shelter, food, and clothing for the family. Little time or thought was given to building a relationship.

Today's marriage is totally relational.

These days couples think more in terms of wanting emotional rather than physical needs met. We want to be valued for what we are, not because we bring home a salary or perform household tasks.

Communication tops everyone's list nowadays because it is basic to intimate relationships. Communication is what sparks caring, giving, sharing, and affirming. Unless we understand and utilise properly the principles of listening and speaking, we can't really know or understand each other. We remain closed to one another.

The husband who walks in the door and says, 'Hi, honey,' which pretty well sums up the evening's conversation, is not demonstrating that he has mastered many communication skills.

A wife who sinks into the silent treatment because her husband said something that hurt her feelings is doing likewise. What each is really showing is that he or she doesn't care enough to risk telling the other who he/she is or what he/she is experiencing each day.

A major reason husband and wife fail to communicate adequately is that they are afraid to share real thoughts and feelings with their mates. Fear of experiencing the ultimate hurt, rejection, blocks open sharing of thoughts and feelings.

'Those who control their tongue will have a long life; opening your mouth can ruin everything.'
Proverbs 13:3

Who hasn't opened up to
a partner and been rebuffed?
Some people get hurt so
badly they refuse to come
back for more. Instead, they
crawl into a shell and stay
there.

'The tongue can bring death or life; those who love to talk will reap the consequences.'
Proverbs 18:21

Talking and listening: both essential to communication.

Some fail to communicate because it is easier to avoid and repress ideas and feelings than it is to learn how to process them properly. This reason is closely connected to how we feel about ourselves. If you think you or your opinions are worthless, why attempt to share them?

Address those self-worth issues!

'A time to be quiet and a time to speak.'
Ecclesiastes 3:7

A vital communication skill is to sense what time it is!

Some couples can't communicate because they have never experienced success at it. Whenever they attempted to open up, they were tuned out or shot down.

Early lessons in protecting our feelings teach us to measure carefully what can and cannot be shared with those we love. As a result, many people live much like turtles: They stick out their heads cautiously for air, only to have them lopped off by predators. Eventually, they spend more time inside than outside their shells.

How you communicate today was influenced by the home you grew up in. While growing up, you carefully observed how family members spoke and responded to one another. This became your model for how people talk, listen and respond.

Your communication patterns may conflict sharply with your partner's. Your family may have settled differences of opinion through quiet discussion. In your partner's family, they may have been settled through loud arguments.

'Get rid of all bitterness, rage, anger, harsh words, and slander, as well as all types of evil behaviour.'
Ephesians 4:31

*'Don't sin by letting anger
control you. Don't let the
sun go down while you
are still angry.'*
Ephesians 4:26

After she gets married, a woman expects intimate and meaningful heart-to-heart talks. Most men don't need heart-to-heart talks but may miss doing things with male friends where activities play a major role.

A man's brain is wired to be more analytical, and a female's to be more intuitive or emotional. Women complain that their husbands won't talk to them, and men complain about how emotional their wives are.

'Don't sin by letting anger control you. Think about it overnight and remain silent.'
Psalm 4:4

Some studies suggest
that more genes are passed
on from grandparents than
parents. This combination
of traits is largely responsible
for your actions, reactions
and emotional responses,
and to a large extent
determines how you
communicate.

Many people get so caught in a web of inadequate communication habits that they give up trying. Multitudes communicate through ineffective, shallow, and hollow methods, never thinking of changing their own patterns of communication.

You may need to change your communication habits!

Ask yourself, What specific changes do you need to make in order to achieve your goal of more effective communication? What changes are you *willing* to make?

Give improving your communication all you've got. No conditional commitments; no exceptions; no fine print; no ifs, ands, or buts; no time limits.

Work at communication whether or not you feel like it – even when your partner breaks all the rules. Resist the inclination to pout, run or punish your spouse when your attempts fail. Simply resolve to work at improving your communication, regardless of any distractions.

'So get rid of all evil behaviour. Be done with all deceit, hypocrisy, jealousy, and all unkind speech.'
1 Peter 2:1

You may be in a rut, but you *can* get out if you are motivated.

Many couples are bonded
but not married; others are
married but suffering from
weak, damaged, or
disintegrating bonds.

Communication, as ever,
is the key.

*'Say only what helps,
each word a gift.'*
Ephesians 4:29b, MGE

Bonding describes the fusing not only of two separate and distinct individual lives but also a blending of their minds, ideas and personalities. Two previously separate and distinct persons now blend their values, goals and beliefs. Their hopes, dreams and futures merge to form one unit.

Do your life goals and personal beliefs blend well? Do you each bring out the best in the other, motivating one another to better and higher challenges and accomplishments? Do you know your partner's expectations of you for the future? Can you fulfil them? Will your partner allow you to develop your talents and be yourself?

'Let your speech at all times be gracious [pleasant and winsome], seasoned [as it were] with salt.' Colossians 4:6, *Amplified Bible.*

There are many factors
which stretch the bond.
The first is separation.

When a couple is well
bonded, brief separations
will not disturb the bond.
However, repeated absences,
when frequent or prolonged,
stretch the capacity of the
best of bonds.

Stress, in its many forms, can weaken a bond. The stress may be caused by a job, finances, fatigue, illness, a rebellious teenager, or any number of other stress-related problems. Extreme fatigue resulting from stress may lessen sexual desire.

Grief can seriously challenge a bond.

Grief which follows divorce, death or abandonment of a spouse, must be worked through before beginning a new relationship. Too often hurting partners rush from one relationship to the next with disastrous consequences.

'Worry weighs a person down; an encouraging word cheers a person up.'
Proverbs 12:25

Time to try harder?

If you and your mate interacted while dating the way you are interacting now, would you like each other and know each other well enough to marry?

If a strong bond is to be maintained, it must be renewed daily.

The bond will disintegrate without constant nurturing, communication and mutual trust.

'Watch your tongue and keep your mouth shut, and you will stay out of trouble.'
Proverbs 21:23

Learn to communicate calmly, reasonably and constructively.

'The tongue is a flame of fire. It is a whole world of wickedness, corrupting your entire body. It can set your whole life on fire, for it is set on fire by hell itself.'
James 3:6

Tongue-control is the most important part of self-control. *And it's a learned skill. . . .*

Communication must be verbal

Unsatisfactory communication skills is one of the easiest characteristics to identify in a crumbling relationship. When a couple communicates unsatisfactorily, they will function poorly as a team.

Some couples talk more but say less. That is because verbalisation for them takes the form of 'speeches'.

Communication involves an easy flow of conversation. Tremendous power struggles may dominate the relationship, along with blaming, judging and put-downs during a time of stress.

Deliver a verbal bouquet

A verbal bouquet is any
affirmation which shows
acceptance, appreciation,
or respect for your partner.

Well-bonded couples have learned to keep the channels of communication open. They tend to listen with respect and accept all feelings, even when they don't agree.

'Let your speech always be with grace, as though seasoned with salt, so that you will know how you should respond to each person.'
Colossians 4:6, NASV

When the lines of communication shut down between two people, it is like a terminal illness, and it is rarely reversible unless the partners work together to halt the dread disease.

Any couple who can master three basic skills of communication – the verbalisation of feelings, attentive listening, and reactive feedback – can save or restore a weak or damaged bond.

Look at each other when you speak. Eye contact is vital. Lack of eye contact and dishonesty go hand in hand.

Touch is also involved in communication.

The adult need for touching is more basic than the need for sex.

Tremendous rewards await any couple who begin weaving the joy of touch into the everyday fabric of their lives. For instance, a couple can join hands during prayer; give a loving pat; hold hands when going for a walk or while riding in the car; cuddle at night with no demands for sex; sit close at church or while watching TV; greet each other with a hug and kiss.

Three hugs a day keep depression away. Touching can stabilise the heart rate of the intensive-care patient; improve movement for cerebral palsy victims; heal the sick by the laying on of hands, as evidenced both in Bible and present times; raise children's grade point averages; activate haemoglobin and brainwave activity.

Why is it that when couples are going out together they can hardly keep their hands off one another, while after marriage they hardly touch except to communicate sexual readiness?

Non-sexual touching is very important.

Women have a tremendous need to be held, aside from sex. It gives them a feeling of emotional satisfaction to be held outside the bedroom. Any woman who associates each touch with a sexual encounter will come to resent it.

Couples who say they have fallen out of love with their mates could rebuild a relationship just by re-initiating loving caresses. Touching can do more to heal the wounds of bickering, hostility and negative attitudes than any treatment modality.

'Let everything you say
be good and helpful, so
that your words will be an
encouragement to those
who hear them.'
Ephesians 4:29b

Verbal communication, eye contact and touching are what keep a marital bond interesting and vital over the long haul.

Make the first four minutes
of contact every morning
and the first four minutes of
contact when you reunite at
the end of the working day
a pleasant interlude.

There are six easy ways to strengthen a bond.

The first is *prepare yourself mentally.*

Think good thoughts. Some people actually *plan* to dump bad feelings on their partners.

Instead of planning in such a negative direction, rehearse in your mind at least one positive incident from your day that you can share with your partner upon greeting him or her.

Pray on the way home that
the Lord will prepare you to
be a blessing to your partner.
Sometimes a quick phone
call in advance helps
prepare the way.

Plan your time so you can greet your partner smiling. Let your partner know he or she is a priority in your life, not someone to be fitted in after other responsibilities have been taken care of.

A smile can say 'I love you' with more meaning than an expensive gift.

Check your appearance.
That, too, is important for
strengthening the bond.

Greet each other with a hug and a kiss.

If kissing isn't your style, have some other physical contact: holding hands, patting, fondling.

Do something that re-establishes touch.

Rather than greeting your partner with 'didyas' – 'Didya go to the bank?' etc. – or a curt hello, greet your partner with some verbal pleasantry. A warm 'welcome home, darling' or a compliment will do.

Before your partner comes home of an evening, make a deliberate attempt to create a pleasant atmosphere.

Give each other time to relax before tackling any problems.

Those who are serious about strengthening their marital bond, or who wish to salvage a deteriorating relationship, must begin with revitalising the crucial eight minutes after the couple is reunited following the day's work. These contact minutes, to a large degree, symbolise how a man and woman have integrated their lives.

With new insights and by carefully structuring these eight minutes a day, a couple can experience a sense of renewal.

Active *listening* is vital to the success of communication

Listening is the most neglected and least understood of the communication arts. Perceptive listening doesn't require a degree, but it does require learning.

In a communication inventory participants were asked to respond to the statement: 'My partner listens attentively to what I have to say.' Forty-seven percent said that their partners listened attentively 'some of the time', 'rarely' or 'never'. Fifty-five percent admitted that their partners accused them of not listening all, most, or part of the time.

'If only you could be silent! That's the wisest thing you could do.'
Job 13:5

Silence is golden – when you are listening actively.

Many of us assume listening is something we do with our ears. Hearing refers to the process by which sound waves hit the ear with lightning speed and are transmitted to the brain – an unlearned process occurring without conscious effort on our part.

Listening, however, describes *a skill which one learns.*

Poor listening stems from bad habits

Interrupting is the number one bad habit. Interrupters spend their time not listening to what is being said but in forming a reply. Interested only in their own ideas, they pay little attention to the words of others and wait for a split second when they can break in.

Lack of eye contact is the second bad listening habit.

Listeners who fail to look at the person speaking to them convey lack of interest, distrust and a want of caring.

The insensitive listener is one who cannot catch the feeling behind the words. A young wife asks her husband to take her out to dinner. She does not need to be taken out to dinner as much as she needs reassurance that he still loves her and is willing to please her. If he tells her bluntly that they can't afford it or he is too tired, he hasn't listened to the meaning behind her request.

Other annoying listening
habits include:
- one who makes you feel
  you are wasting his time;
- pacing back and forth as
  if impatient or in a hurry to
  get away;
- no facial expressions
  indicating understanding
  or hearing;

- pre-stating your point or pre-finishing your sentences;
- rephrasing what you say so that words are put in your mouth;
- asking a question to which you've just given the answer;
- contradicting what you say before you even state your case;
- standing too close.

Listening involves more than hearing words. It involves discernment, observing non-verbals, caring, eye contact, watching for underlying motives, asking the right questions, giving appropriate responses, and sometimes being silent.

Practise total body listening:

Look like a listener.

Total body listening can be described as an activity in which you utilise every part of your body to show your partner you are listening.

Listen with your eyes

Look at the person who is
speaking to you. Make sure
your partner senses you are
listening.

Listen with your head

Unless you nod your head in agreement, there is little motivation for the speaker to continue. Resting a forefinger on the side of your face, head in hand, indicates thoughtful listening.

Listen with your hands

Hands are capable of
many gestures which can
communicate approval or
disapproval.

Avoid doodling or drawing
pictures while you are listening.
Fidgeting with paperclips
or pencils and clipping or
cleaning fingernails are
silent but often hurtful and
frustrating nuisances which
say, 'You aren't as important
to me as this is.'

The human touch is vital to emotional health

Touching shows we are paying attention. Touch heals, lifts up, affirms others and conveys a message that can't be expressed in words.

Listen with your body

We convey either openness
or defensiveness through
body postures. The gesture
for defensiveness is arms
folded across the chest.
In contrast, arms
outstretched, palms up,
indicates openness and
sincerity.

Listen with your mouth

Mouth listening includes smiling, laughter, a low whistle, a light kiss, and other ways the mouth might be used to show caring.

Listen with your mind

Intentional listening searches for thoughts, intentions and action statements as well.

You need to develop deliberate listening skills for banking information.

Match your listening responses to your partner's behaviour. While not mimicking your partner's behaviour, match your body language to his or hers.

If your partner is happy and excited about something, adapt your total body listening to a spirit of joy.

We can think five times faster than we can talk. That means that there is 'lag time' as you listen to someone else's contribution to the conversation. Unless you pay attention during the lag time, you'll catch only a portion of what your mate is saying.

Learn not to tune out.

A good listening technique is found in responding with a 'door opener' or the invitation to say more. The simplest door openers are 'Great!' or 'I understand'. More explicit door openers are 'That sounds interesting! Tell me more,' or 'I can see how important this is to you.'

Practise creative questioning

Creative questioning is really a listening rather than a speaking skill since you would be unable to phrase an appropriate question unless you have been listening.

Body language: do actions speak louder than words?

All body responses and emotional expressions are part of non-verbal communication – a silent persuasion that tells the real story.

Few people grasp the
importance of non-verbals.
In normal communication,
the words used or content
accounts for only 7% of what
is conveyed. Tone of voice
and gestures amount to
38%; facial expressions
alone account for an
astonishing 55%.

*A total of 93% of what
is communicated is
done without words.*

All body positions either support or deny a verbal message. Sagging shoulders communicate discouragement; slouching in a chair, lack of interest; head in hands, despair; a shrug of the shoulders, 'I don't know'; a rigid position, tension; crossed arms, defiance.

Eyes are the most expressive part of facial expressions. Their shiftiness, narrowing, widening, a slow roll, dullness, and rate of blinking all tell the mood of their owner.

Gestures are part of body language. The outstretched arm with palm up demonstrates openness and acceptance; the outstretched arm, palm down, indicates closure and distance.

Dress is an obvious aspect of body language. 'Loud' clothes beg for attention; sloppy clothes indicate carelessness; immodest clothes, a desperate plea for attention.

Voice cues

Words convey information, but how those words are spoken – volume, speed, inflection and emphasis – carries more weight. The teasing tone, the touch of humour, judgemental chastisement, convey friendliness, happiness or anger. Cues tell the other person whether to come closer or back off.

Speech mannerisms

Attitudes, meanings and emotions are communicated through a variety of mannerisms. The 'yes, but' speech mannerism is from a person who habitually contradicts. The 'I know' mannerism conveys 'You dummy! You can't teach me anything I don't know already.'

Learn to develop a sensitivity to non-verbals

Consciously practise recognising body, voice and emotional cues.

Learn to recognise a 'mixed message'

When a person's words say one thing and his body language or tone of voice another, it is a mixed message. Since tone of voice and body language make up 93% of the message, they are more believable than the words.

By paraphrasing what the speaker said, the listener can clarify the accuracy of a statement. Paraphrasing can unmuddle the muddled.

But unlike active listening, paraphrasing deals only with information shared, not with feelings.

Clarifying what has been said is important in all relationships, but especially in marriage.

Many misunderstandings which begin innocently could be avoided if the listener would only check on whether his perception was clear.

The most deadly killer message of all is the silent treatment. To clam up, withdraw, retreat, refuse to talk about something, or hide behind a curtain of hurt, does more to clog communication than any other killer message. It has been said that adultery slays its thousands but silence its tens of thousands.

A soft voice can reassure and comfort a hurting partner. It says, 'I'm here. I care and understand.'

Scripture backs up this assertion: *'A soft answer turneth away wrath.'* Proverbs 15:1, KJV

Most people would prefer a good argument to silence – at least they get feedback. If you want your partner to resent you and possibly leave, talk only when you feel like it, pay little attention when your partner is speaking, and use silence frequently!

Morning moods

Some people awake early in the morning ready to set the world on fire. Others resent wake-up calls prior to 9am and even then present themselves puffy-eyed and grumpy. I have not yet figured out why such people marry each other, but I do know the early bird will not endear himself to his partner by chirping each morning at 6am.

All five communication levels are useful and necessary in maintaining relationships, but communication on the deep-insight level is a must for couples today. Couples of yesteryear could survive in a 'functional marriage' without it. But today's 'relational marriage' requires a depth beyond functionality.

Use I-messages

Sending an I-message is a
method of expressing your
feelings directly when upset,
irritated or annoyed by
your partner's behaviour.
I-messages let your partner
know you have negative
feelings about the behaviour,
but you do not attack or
ridicule. Rather than
attacking, say, 'I feel
irritated when you . . .
because . . .'

Always ask yourself, *Are my words distancing or drawing?*

An I-message rather than
a you-message exemplifies
the difference between
assertiveness and
aggressiveness. An assertive
individual can speak the
truth concerning his feelings
without blaming the other
person. Aggression clobbers
your partner with your
feelings in a hostile
        manner.

A major goal of the I-message
is to release your feelings of
irritation. Your partner may
or may not change his
behaviour, but you are
staying in touch with your
feelings and communicating
them in a direct way rather
than suppressing them.

Unattended little resentments
and irritations can fester into
big, bitter fights.

His and hers

Male and female just may be marching to different drummers. Misunderstandings resulting from a lack of knowledge about male-female talk styles can lead to frustration and misery.

Rather than assuming something is wrong with your partner when you come up with different conclusions, why not accept these differences as part of God's marvellous plan for male and female.

Talk time

Taking time to talk means
sharing positive experiences
and ideas, not just criticisms,
worries or arguments.

A couple who talks little
today sets the stage for more
difficulty in talking tomorrow.

Tough stuff for wives

*'It's better to live alone
in the desert than with
a quarrelsome,
complaining wife.'*
Proverbs 21:19

*'A quarrelsome wife is
as annoying as constant
dripping on a rainy day.'*
Proverbs 27:15

Important stuff for husbands

'Husbands, . . . love your wives just as Christ loved the church. He gave up his life for her.'
Ephesians 5:25

'Husbands, love your wives and never treat them harshly.'
Colossians 3:19

'You must all be quick to listen, slow to speak, and slow to get angry. Human anger does not produce the righteousness God desires.'
James 1:19, 20

So talk!

- Work at talking. Make time to talk, and create things to talk about.

- Maintain a daily talk time. Set aside time each day to talk about non-controversial marriage matters.

- Observe the marriage meeting. Ideally, once or twice a week a couple should have a set, previously-agreed-upon time when family business is discussed. Problems are solved at this time, decisions regarding family plans are discussed, and schedules for the forthcoming week are co-ordinated.

We have the ability to heal or hurt one another, restore or deplete, to help or hinder. We can make our mates feel important, alive and worthy, or we can make them feel inadequate and useless.

Let us move in a positive direction.